SMALL BUSINESS

The Most Important Things you Need to Know to Create and Grow a Successful Small Business from Scratch

Contents

Introduction

I want to congratulate you on purchasing this book. You have just taken the first step to starting your own business. If you purchased this book you are probably in your 20s, 30s or 40s and are fed up with your current job. You are probably tired of living life on everybody else's terms. You can change that. You can start your own business and live the life you want. You can have the life that you deserve!

This book will teach you how to start a business in 4 easy steps.

1. Come up with a business idea. We'll
    cover different ways to come up with
    that idea and how to research it.

2. Reduce your expenses. Let's be realistic,
    you're going to have to take a financial
    hit when you first start your business.
    There is no way around it. You need to
    prepare ahead of time for this.

3. Make some money fast. You need to
    figure out a quick way to start making
    money outside of your current job that
    doesn't take up a lot of your time. The
    idea is to bring in some cash so that you
    can quit your job but to be able to spend
    most of your time on your business.
    We'll discuss some techniques on how
    you can do this.

4. Quit your job and work full time on your business. We'll discuss when the right time is to leave your job.

The above 4 steps work, but don't be confused they are far from easy. If starting a business were easy then everyone would do it. You are going to have to really think outside of the box, get out of your comfort zone and push yourself to make this happen. I know you can do it and I'm here to help.

Thank you and good luck!

John Robert

Chapter 1. The Idea

Starting a business seems to be a daunting prospect, but it can be the perfect chance to prove yourself. You will get a chance to do anything that you would like to. That means that you can focus your energy into your passions, rather than having to live and breathe another person's dream. Working for yourself means more than a paycheck, because you get that chance to create something of value that people will want to pay for.

The ability to create is not something that just happens without work though. You can't just sit down with a paper and pen and expect an idea to just appear. Well okay, this does happen for some people, like Mark Zuckerberg creating Facebook, but even this took planning and a no small amount of work. You want to try to find a niche that works well for you. You want to find a business idea that suits your strengths.

To prepare to break into the niche field that you have selected you should start with research. There are quite a few resources you can use for your research. You should study blogs as they can give you a great deal of insight into what different people are doing in your area business. Also listen to podcasts, as they will contain a good amount of information from interviews with other self-employed individuals, and they can be uplifting, or inspiring to hear the success stories of others.

Search Engines results will give you a great way to find new information about your business, and the product or service that you want to offer. The search engine results will also direct you to emerging competition, and additional research that you may need to break into your niche. You can also read, there are a variety of books that will help you in your chosen business area.

Finally it is important to find a mentor. They will be able to provide you with insight that you may have otherwise missed. All the research in the world can't give you the experience and real life knowledge that a mentor can. You should find someone that is happy to answer your questions and can be an encouraging influence on your budding business.

Blogs

The blogosphere is a phrase that makes you think of another world that writes and critiques all things on this little marble we call Earth. The World Wide Web contains many such blogs, but there is also a wealth of knowledge from people just like you contained in blogs. This is why you should read them. These are other people just like you who have similar interests and can help you on your way to saying goodbye to your boss. Remember a blog can be written to help others, provide knowledge and function as a public journal or window into the lives of others.

Reading blogs can help you to become your own boss and learn what it was like for others who started where you are now. It will help you to understand what the plunge will be like when you do decide to leave your job. Blogs can also provide a good resource to see how well your niche is covered by others and how well you will be able to compete. Blogs can also give you some insight on your target customers. Will your product or service meet their needs?

Let's go back to the journal blog types, they may seem secondary when you are looking for information to start your own business, but there is a great deal of information that is freely given in these blogs. This is especially true if you are not sure what type of product or service to bring to market. You can do market research just by reading about the everyday problems or gripes that those with a blog have. This can give you ideas in what type of product you should bring to market. Whether it be a service to fill a perceived gap or a product to help others be more productive.

Podcasts

Podcasts are a great learning resource because of the ability to listen to a piece by piece library of information. When you are trying to get your business plan together it can be a daunting task. This is why podcasts are perfect to begin learning about your area of business. You can listen to them on your mp3 player, iPod or phone while in the car, on the bus or between classes if you are in college. They are great for when you are on the move but still want to work on your business ideas. They are also great for finding some inspiration toward your goals.

They allow you to focus on the information without having to be tied to a book or computer. The piece by piece nature of podcast also gives you the advantage of breaking down much larger chunks of information for running a business into manageable and learnable portions. This will make the ideas that you hear easy to remember and you can always reference them just by listening to the episode again.

Podcasts can also inspire new ideas. Even if the podcast is not directly related to your business idea, it may give you some insight into how to improve your product or service. When you are passionate about your business idea, you will find that learning more will give you a better edge and make the overall idea flow more efficiently. There are some great resources available in the business podcast arena, such as *Starting from Nothing* by The Foundation, and *The Startup Business Podcast* that is produced by startupbusiness.com.

Search Engines

Everyone who uses the internet today is familiar with at least one of these internet search giants. We type in our question and the search engine returns us links to the content we are looking for. Earlier we discussed podcasts and blogs but without starting with a search engine you will not be able to find the content you need.

As the owner of your own business it is vital that you stay on top of the news and information in your market niche and using a search engine such as Google or Yahoo will give you the ability to find relevant content quickly. In the beginning this will be most likely how you find information about your target customers, your possible product or service and even how to market it to your customers.

Another great thing about the search engines is that they will list products in their ad space on either side of the main links that can give you an idea if there are other products or services that are already in existence for your business idea. It is always good to learn what the competition has been up to and what they are offering. It is also important to check these products because you do not want to try to sell the same idea and end up with a copyright issue.

The search engine is also something you will want to keep in mind when it comes time to monetize your plan. Money is the name of the game! Let's not get ahead of the master plan though, we will discuss that in a later chapter.

Books

With all the technology in the world, it is easy to forget that the good old printed book is still out there waiting to be thumbed through (or for those who would rather save paper, eBook clicked though!). There is a wealth of information that you can learn from books. They will give you ideas of products, services and even how to create a sound business plan. The book you are holding now is one such book that will give you advice on how be free of the constant grind of a job, be your own boss and build your own business.

So what kinds of books should you read? Well this is going to be more up to you. What is your idea? Are there any books about what you want to offer the world? Some recommendations to read would be about how to run a business. Many people launch a business without knowing what it will take to be the owner and leader of their own business. It is important to read into how to register your new business and how to pay the government their share if you are wildly successful. As important as the nuts and bolts of a company are, there is another very important factor that books can help you with.

They can help you with finding your target customers. There are several books about how to reach out to your customers, meet them on their level and show them your product is for them. Many of these books will be more about behavior and how to see from a customer's perspective. One book that I recommend is

<u>Traction Book – The Guide to Getting Customers</u> by Gabriel Weinberg and Justin Mare. It is a good read and both these authors started where you are now so they know first-hand what it takes to build a successful business.

Mentor

Sometimes all the reading and research in the world just can't help you get the ball rolling and that is perfectly okay. So what do you do next? You find someone doing the same thing you want to do and you connect with them. Reach out to them and let them know that you want to learn more about how they got their business up and running. Don't be shy, let them know that you want to leave the workforce and start your own company. Most self-made individuals are perfectly willing to lend a hand and some valuable advice. If they are too busy to help you see if they have a book you can purchase and read. Even better, see if they have a blog!

Remember people are people, even business owners. Some may not respond to you or may respond negatively. You may have caught them on a bad day, who knows? They key is don't give up. Reach out to others and you will certainly find someone who is willing to give you some advice with your business. Try to do something to help them out too. Don't just ask them for advice and give them nothing in return.

If they are selling a product, purchase the product and make a testimonial for them. Ask them if there is anything you can do to help them. Maybe they need help purchasing a new TV and you're a TV expert. It doesn't have to be related to business necessarily. You're relationship with a mentor has to be give and take. At first you have to be the one doing most of the giving and only taking a little. As your relationship grows you can expect more and more from your mentor.

Chapter 2. Reduce Expenses

So you want to quit your job and get your dream business off the ground? How are you going to live and support yourself until your idea begins to make money? This can be a hard question when you begin to think about launching your business and quitting your full time job. It is daunting to not know where your next paycheck is going to come from. With a full time job, you get a regular paycheck that you can count on to pay your bills. When you run your own business, you aren't always sure when you will get paid next. You may not get paid at all during the beginning months. To be successful as a new business owner you should consider a few ways to reduce your bills and even explore some unique ways to make some side cash while you launch your business. After all, you will need to invest both time and money into your company.

Move In With Family or Friends

This can be somewhat challenging to your independent lifestyle. It can be extremely hard to take a step back and move back in with your parents or a relative after making it on your own for so long. There is no question about it; this is an excellent way to reduce your expenses. If you can manage to live with a family member rent free, not having to pay rent regularly means that you will have that much extra cash to invest in your business idea. It is not that uncommon for those in their twenties and thirties to live with their parents in this day in age.

It is also not uncommon for adults in their 40s and 50s to be living with other family members. Jobs are harder to come by and usually your parents or relatives will understand. They should support your decision to start your own business that is what family is supposed to do. Just ask them, they may even be willing to help you get the business started. You might have some tasks that are really hard to do on your own that they might be able to help you with. They may also be able to provide you with advice and experience that you may not have had the opportunity to get yet.

Some people may not have family they are able to move in with to reduce their expenses. That is okay, there is still hope! You might have a close friend, girlfriend / boyfriend or husband / wife that can help you out. Your friend may let you crash on their couch for a few months while you build your business up. Maybe your girlfriend or husband may be willing to pay the bills while you build up the business. You have to be willing to ask people. A lot of people really want to help but you never know if you don't ask. You may feel like you owe the person big time and that's okay, there will be a time in the future where you can repay them somehow. The key is to let them help you now and focus on your business.

An alternative to moving in with a family member or friend is to roommate with other people. This will not save you as much money as living rent free but it will split them up among multiple people which makes it a lot more affordable. A lot of times you can find people on a site like Craigslist who are looking for a roommate for only a couple hundred dollars a month. They may have an extra room in their house that they may just want to rent out and get some money coming in to help them pay bills. You may also have a friend who has an extra room in their house.

If you absolutely don't feel comfortable asking them if you can live with them rent free, offer them a few hundred a month to live there. If they have a spare room they may need the cash and may have never even thought of the idea themselves. It could end up being a win / win situation for the both of you. If you decide that you want to start this business with other people you could all move into a really cheap place together and split the cost. This could end up being a win / win situation too because you'll be able to work on the business all the time together.

Just remember that going into business with another person means that all partners are responsible for the future of the business. This could be a good thing or a bad thing depending on your feelings and your potential partners. You may not want the future of the business in their hands.

Pay Down, Refinance or Defer Student Loans

Another way to reduce expenses is to take a look at your student loans. Most adults in their twenties, thirties, forties and even fifties may have racked up quite a large amount in student loans that they are still paying back. Student loan debt is no joke and those monthly payments can be staggering. Unless you have a degree and job in a well-paying field, you may already be struggling to pay your student loans every month.

This right off the bat may deter you from quitting your job to start a business. If you can barely afford to pay your student loans now, how will you afford to pay them when you don't even know when you will be getting paid next? If your goal is to quit your job and start a business then you need to figure out how to lower or eliminate these payments when you are starting out. The good news is there are some ways.

The first option is to try to eliminate them or reduce them significantly while you still have your job. You may be doing research now on how to start a business but you may not want to actually quit your job for another 6 - 18 months and that's okay. Make extra payments against the principle of your student loans. This will reduce the interest that they gain, and can help you to pay them off quicker. If you can't afford to do that with what you are currently making from your job, get a second job for a year while you are planning out your business. No one said this was going to be easy! If you want to quit your job tomorrow and start your business then this isn't going to be appealing to you.

There are some other options. A second option is to consolidate your loans to get a better interest rate and lengthen the amount of time you have to pay them off. This will reduce your monthly payment in the short term and once your business is making some good money you can start paying more towards your student loans to pay them off faster.

There is also one more option if you absolutely just cannot afford to have any type of school loan payment while you are starting your business. You can attempt to get a forbearance or deferment. This means that your student loan payment will be placed on hold for a period of time. The only downside to this is that interest still accrues while you are deferring the payment. It may just be a sacrifice you have to make. One last option is going back to school at least part time while starting your business. This will place your loans back into forbearance while you are taking classes. The nice thing about this is that as long as you are registered at least part time as a student then your loans will stay in forbearance. You will have to pay these loans back eventually and you may not even have a desire to actually get another degree.

These are the two downsides to this option. If you have no desire to get a degree I'd recommend just going to a local community college that has extremely cheap tuition. You can take two easy classes there that will not take up a lot of your time but that will allow you to put your school loan payment back on deferment. After your business is up, running and making a profit paying back your student loans should be no problem!

Cash Out 401K

So you have figured out a way to reduce your living expenses and school loans but you still need some capital to launch your business. Where are you going to get it? Should you take out a loan? The answer is no, do not take out a loan for your business. The first option I recommend is cashing out your 401K retirement savings account. I know a lot of you will think it's crazy to do this, but just follow me for a minute. Your 401K is normally for your retirement and yes you will take a big tax hit if you cash it out early. You will also not have any retirement savings to fall back on when you get older, so why am I recommending you do this then? You want to quit your job that you hate and start your dream business, your life's work.

This is something that you should love doing and will want to do for the rest of your life.

Your business is also an investment. Instead of letting some mutual fund manager handle your money you can now be in control of how much your money can make for you. If you invest $5,000 into your business, you may be able to get back your initial investment plus another $5,000. That is a 100% return on investment. If you can do that in a year's time there is no way the person who is managing the mutual fund that your 401K savings is in can match that! Most people don't even understand what their money is doing in their 401K savings account anyways. You have to remember what your goal is and that money that you have set aside in a 401K may not be making you much money at all. Cash it out, and use that money to launch your business. Yes, you will pay a penalty on the funds, but it is worth getting that money in a liquid form so you can use it as you need for your business.

Remember you will have to pay the tax penalty, and this is not an excuse to not save money for later in life. Once your company is up and running you will want to make plans to start saving again. The goal is to be making more money from your business than you were with your job and to love what you are doing. If you are making more money from your business that means you have more money to save. One last thing, don't think of cashing out your 401K as a bonus or extra money. You must use it exclusively on your business. You are making an investment here in your businesses future profitability.

Eliminate or Negotiate Bills

At this point we got living expenses, school loans and startup money take care of. The last things we have to worry about are our monthly bills. They usually come every month and you most likely have more than one! Not to fear, we can find a way to reduce these bills down to something manageable. If you intend to quit your job to become your own boss and run your own business, then it is more important than ever to analyze how you spend your money and find ways to trim the budget down to something you are comfortable with and give you the extra breathing room you will need.

We have already addressed your living situation. This alone can be a huge money saver if you don't have to pay rent and utilities every month. If you are just rooming with someone and still have to pay water, electricity, television, gas, and internet charges you will need to look into ways to reduce those or even eliminate them based on your circumstances. You may want to get rid of cable but your roommates may not.

This can be a dilemma but maybe you can work out a deal with your roommates that since they want it and you don't that they have to pay for it. There are also some tactics I don't necessarily recommend but can use if you a desperate. For example, usually if you pay a portion of your utility bill but not the full amount they will not shut you off. You can usually call and negotiate this with the utility company too. They may be willing to accept a lower payment for 6 months while you get your business going. Some of you may be appalled at the thought of not paying your bill in full and I completely understand.

It isn't the best decision but if you truly desire to start your own business and have no other options to pay your bills then it's something that you can do. They usually won't report this kind of stuff to the credit card reporting agencies as long as you are making some type of payment. This would definitely be something to ask them about though as you don't want to ruin your credit.

 Now let's talk about cell phones. That Smart phone that you have in your pocket, are you getting the best rate for your service? Do you think you could call and negotiate a better deal? I'm willing to bet you probably could. Most cell phone carriers don't want to lose you as a customer and if you call up and tell them you want to leave for a cheaper service provider they will most likely offer you a discount. Even if the first time you try this it doesn't work, call again later and try again.

Sometimes this type of thing just depends on who you talk to on the phone and what kind of day they are having. These are the type of things you want to be thinking about though. Even if they refuse to lower your monthly bill you can probably really go out and find another cheaper company to go with. It may suck to have to change cell phones but it will be worth it if you can get a lower monthly payment while still ensuring that you get the needed services.

Now for personal expenses, as a young adult you may like to go out on the town. Having some time to live it up is an excellent way to unwind and relax. How much do you spend on an evening out though? Since you are becoming a business owner, it is time to think about that money in your wallet as the asset it is.

Is it worth giving that asset up for dinner and drinks at the bar? Would a Netflix movie and a cheap bottle of wine with friends give you the same good time? Can you cook? Maybe you could throw a bash at your house and do some grilling instead. You could tell everyone to bring a dish and bring their own alcohol.

If you have a gym membership, could you just run outside instead? Little expenses that you don't think of like coffee, that bag of chips at the gas station and fast food can add up quickly. It sucks to have to worry about that kind of stuff but if you are trying to start a business it is important to keep track of those expenditures. The $100 you save per month by cutting out those types of little purchases can pay your cell phone bill for the month.

It's not a lot but trust me when you first get started in business every penny counts. Remember to be successful running your own business you must make a profit. It can take time to make enough profit to be able to pay yourself so you have to budget your money extremely carefully.

Save! Save! Save!

If you have a job right now, then the first step to quitting your job and running your own business is to save enough money to live on comfortably while you get your business started. Most experts recommend six months' salary in the bank, in case it takes that long to start turning a profit. To help save this amount, you can follow the steps outlined in the previous sections, which will help you find more money in your budget on a regular basis.

Take any extra cash you have while still working your job and place it in a high yield savings account. If you plan on working for 6 months or longer a Certificate of Deposit could be a better option.

A CD is a great short term savings option. It usually gives you a higher interest rate than a savings account and it locks your money up where you can't be tempted to withdraw it for a certain period of time. You won't get rich from the interest you make from a CD but it will give you something which will add to your pool of usable monetary resources.

Chapter 3. Make Money Fast

So here we are, now it's time to start taking action towards starting your own business. You have an idea; you have reduced your expenses and increased your money supply through savings. You've taken the necessary steps to put yourself in a situation where you are finally ready to get the ball moving. So what is your first move? We need to go back to your business idea and figure out the FASTEST way for you to start making some money. This doesn't have to be what your ultimate vision of what your business will be; it just has to be something that you can take action on immediately that will generate you profits fast.

Long Term and Short Term Planning

If you haven't created a full business plan yet for your idea now would be the time to do that as well. You want to create short term and long term goals for your business and a plan on how to achieve them. This doesn't have to be a fancy fifty page document for investors. This just needs to be something simple that you can understand and follow. It could literally be as simple as this.

I will produce [insert product] by [insert how you will make the product] and sell it by [insert how you will sell it]. This will cost me [insert amount] and I will profit [insert amount]. So let's say you wanted to create and sell mugs. You would write this down. I will produce mugs by ordering them from a mug manufacturer and sell them on Amazon and Ebay. It will cost me $1 for each mug and I will sell them for $10 which will give me $5 profit after Amazon / Ebay fees and my cost of the mug. See what I mean? You can do this for both short term and long term goals. So a long term goal might be to sell all different types of glassware. You can break down your long term goals into short term goals by using the formula I provided above.

Let's get back to figuring out the fastest way to make money. We need to take one of the short term goals you created and take action on it immediately. If one of your short term goals is to sell mugs on Amazon and Ebay then we need to do some research to see how mugs are currently selling on both platforms.

We need to make sure that people want to buy mugs, and that they want to actually buy mugs on both Amazon and Ebay. Don't just ask friends and family if they will buy it, most likely they will just say yes because they don't want to upset you. You can purchase some online surveys for a really affordable price that can give you some great insights. You can also do some research on Amazon and Ebay themselves to see if mugs are selling. One of the reasons I'm using Amazon and Ebay as an example is because they are platforms that you can sell your goods on immediately to make fast cash. Your business idea might not be to sell a product but a service.

For example, maybe you want to start a dog walking business. A way you could do research on that business is to put up flyers on telephone poles advertising and see if anyone calls. You may not actually have the service setup yet but if you get some phone calls you know there is a market for the service. You could also just go knock on people's doors that have dogs and ask them. I know this is really uncomfortable but it is a great way to really find out if people would want your service.

The key is that you want to take massive action and fast. We are trying to figure out the quickest way to make a profit. We need to do some quick research and then go out and hustle!

So if your goal is to start a dog care business and you decide one of your short term goals is to offer dog walking as a service you need to go out, put up flyers, knock on doors and sell, sell, sell! Don't be shy or embarrassed about this. Remember, the faster you can start making a profit with your business the better your life is going to be.

Quick Cash Techniques

If you are out there hustling, knocking on doors and frustrated as hell because you're not getting any sales I have some advanced techniques for you to make some quick money. These techniques maybe not be related to your business idea but they can make you some quick cash while you are out there hustling!

Remember those two websites I mentioned earlier, Ebay and Amazon? Well you can sell anything on them! New and used stuff! It's easy as hell to get started selling on them too. It only takes 10 minutes to sign up for an account and get started. You can list items for sale on both Ebay and Amazon and have them sold within minutes! It usually doesn't happen that quickly but realistically you can sell items on both websites within a few days to a few weeks which could bring you in some quick profit while you are building your business.

You might be thinking that you don't have anything to sell. Well I'm going to tell you where you can find stuff to sell. Go to your local thrift store or flea market. They are filled with TONS of items that you can sell on both Amazon and Ebay and make a profit. You can also go to some local garage sales and buy items to sell. The cool thing is that you can even look the items up on your smartphone before you buy them to see if they are worth anything!

Another strategy is to sign up on a freelance website and offer some type of service to people. Some sites where you can do this are odesk.com, fiverr.com and elance.com. You can get paid on these sites to do a ton of different things. Some people might just want you to write them a few blog posts. Others might want you to do some internet research for them. There are literally hundreds of different things you can do to make money on these sites.

One last option (if you already quit your full time job) is to get a part time job while you are working on your business. This can actually be something fun if you want it to be. For example, maybe you always wanted to be a bartender? You could bartend on the weekends and make decent money. You could also use this as an opportunity to learn a skill that could help you in your business.

For example, if you want to start a dog care company you could go work for pet store or a veterinarian. This could be something you line up before you even quit your full time job to ensure you still have cash coming in while you grow your business. You don't have to look at this as a "step down" look at is as more of a side step to reaching your goal of running your own business.

Let's get back to your actual business! Now that you're making some side cash selling on Amazon and Ebay you want to make sure that you are still focused and working hard on your actual business. After you get a few sales your confidence will grow. You will probably make a ton of mistakes during this period too. That is okay, just look at them as learning experiences!

Being a new business owner means that you will find yourself regularly researching the mistakes you made and finding ways to correct them. It is important to remember that you can do this! You have the smarts, the motivation and the skills to be successful with your own business. It just takes time, patience and a good understanding of how to give your customers what they need.

Speaking of customers, you want to make sure that you are providing as much value to them as you can. Every sale you make you want to make sure you are going above and beyond what they expect of you to ensure they have a positive experience.

The more value you can provide the more your customers will trust you. The more they trust you the more they will buy from you. Even if down the line you do make a mistake, if the customer trusts you they will understand and continue to support you. We are all humans and make mistakes. That is why it is important to provide value and build relationships with your customers.

Chapter 4. Quit Your Job

Now the topic you have been waiting for, unless you skipped straight to it of course! When should you quit your full time job to work on your business full time? This is a personal question and is usually best answered by taking a look at your finances and deciding how your time and money can best suit you. There is also something to be said about taking a "leap of faith" as well. If you truly believe in yourself and that you will be successful in your business than by all means quit your job and go after your dreams. There is also nothing wrong with staying at your job and launching your business slowly over time.

Review the section where I talk about making money fast and see if any of those ideas sound appealing to you. You might be able to make enough money with one of those strategies than you can afford to quit your job so that you can spend majority of your time on your business. The one thing you have to really think about is what will work best for you. Some people can work a full time job and launch a business. Some people may need to just focus 100% on the business to be able to make it successful. Figure out which type of person you are and then go with it. In your heart you will know when it's time to quit. You might be scared to do it but you'll have that nagging feeling that just won't go away. That is the sign that you are ready.

It is also important to realize that quitting your job to start a business is a risk. Some risks pay off and some do not. You have to be willing to accept that. Your original business idea might turn out to be a dud. You may have to change course on the fly and try a different one. This is normal. Most successful business owners faced a lot of setbacks before they succeeded. If early on you struggle just remember that. Once you do finally quit your job you will be filled with excitement but as soon as that first setback comes you will be second guessing your decision. Stay positive and keep pushing, this is normal. Just keep making progress and do not quit! You will eventually succeed.

Another thing is that a lot of people will probably think you are crazy for quitting your job to start a business. You have to be willing to accept that too. They will also try to give you all kinds of advice on how to do things. Only listen to people who you feel are truly qualified to give you advice, meaning they are someone who has actually done what they are talking about. If you try to listen to everyone else you will end up getting nowhere.

One last point about quitting your job, don't burn bridges. If you are leaving your company, try to leave on good terms and give proper notice. Some of the people you previously worked with could become your future customers. You could also end up doing business with your previous employer. You never really know what can happen in the future, it is always better to leave everything on better terms than started!

Long Term Vision

Now let's talk about your long term vision for your business. This is the vision that you had all along of where you would eventually like to take your business. We're not just thinking quick cash and in the short term here. What are you going to need to reach your goals and get your business to where you would like it to be? Do you need a web site? Social media profiles? Do you need an office? Will you need outside help? These are all questions that you should be asking yourself as you grow your business and strive towards reaching your ultimate vision. If your plan is to get BIG, you may want to start looking into investors to pitch in or a crowd source funding to get things underway. It is also time to look realistically at where you see your business in 5 - 10 years.

Make sure that you keep things simple at first; you do not want to add complication to the mix until you are firmly established. You don't have to reach your ultimate vision of your business anytime soon. You just want to make sure you know the directions you want to head and take baby steps towards it. Make sure you listen to your customers too. They will be the ones who will show you potential problems that you didn't even know existed. This feedback is extremely valuable and will aid you in reaching your long term goals.

Believe In Yourself!

The most important part of quitting your job and starting a business of your own is belief in yourself! You can have everything else figure out but if you don't truly believe that you can actually make this happen, you won't. If you believe in yourself, you will eventually be successful. There is no doubt about it.

Belief is what is going to get you through working the long hours and doing the dirty work to get your business up and running. Negative thinking can ruin your business before you even start it. I'd definitely recommend making sure your mindset is right before deciding to embark on this journey. It is normal to have some doubts but if you are outright telling yourself "I can't do this", then you won't. You are what you think, as simple as that may sound it is the truth.

You also have to have passion for what you do. If you don't then you will not have the motivation to see it through. Being your own boss and starting your own business sounds great, but make sure that you are doing something you truly love and care about. If you don't have passion for what you are doing it will be difficult to make it through all the struggles and all the hard work that starting a successful business requires.

In the end you will find that being your own boss is infinitely more enjoyable than any job someone else can provide. There is never an ideal time to start your own business.

The best time to do it is now, while you are still young, while you are still full of life! You don't want to be old and on your death bed with regrets! The satisfaction you will get from actually doing it is something you will never regret. It is an amazing feeling to be able to provide tangible value to the world. So quit reading and get started! Today is the day you go out and get started on your business!

Conclusion

After reading this book you may be thinking to yourself "This all sounds great but there is no way this would work for me". You're also probably thinking something along the lines of "There is absolutely NO WAY I can reduce my expenses any more than I already have". I understand that some of what was explained is this book may sound crazy or outlandish. I'm sure if you ask any financial planner in the world if cashing out your 401K is a smart idea they will scream. These strategies aren't for everybody.

These strategies are for people who are willing to try something different. These are for people who are willing to travel down the less traveled road. These are for the people who are willing to grind, get dirty and do whatever it takes.

If you can change your thinking, you can change your life. That is what this book is about. You have to be willing to think about problems differently if you want to be a successful business owner. When you start coming up with creative ideas like the ones mentioned in this book on your own, you will then have the proper mindset to start your own business.

Even if you think every strategy given in this book is ridiculous, I challenge you to come up with your own path. I challenge you to figure out a way RIGHT NOW to be able to quit your job and start a business of your own. Don't limit your thinking in any way. Let your imagination run wild and think of endless possibilities. Somewhere inside your mind is the way to freedom, and it is up to you to find it.